THE BOOK OF

Aloha

Editor's note: All quotations herein are reproduced with the same use (or non-use) of Hawaiian diacriticals as they appeared in their original sources. Therefore, the use of diacriticals are inconsistent.

ISBN-10: 1-56647-985-1
ISBN-13: 978-1-56647-985-1
Library of Congress Control Number: 2012942447

Design by Jane Gillespie
First Printing, September 2012
Second Printing, July 2013
Third Printing, December 2014
Fourth Printing, September 2015
Fifth Printing, December 2016
Sixth Printing, June 2018
Seventh Printing, March 2020

Mutual Publishing, LLC
1215 Center Street, Suite 210
Honolulu, Hawai'i 96816
Ph: (808) 732-1709
Fax: (808) 734-4094
e-mail: info@mutualpublishing.com
www.mutualpublishing.com

Printed in South Korea

THE BOOK OF

Aloha

A Collection of Hawaiian Proverbs & Inspirational Wisdom

Mutual Publishing

Honolulu Star-Bulletin, *unknown*

Introduction

*A*loha can be said to be the soul of Hawai'i, the thread that ties together the Hawaiian cultural and social values that make these Islands so unique. It can be considered the gift of the Hawaiian people to the world daily received and practiced by all who live or visit here. Long after returning home one remembers not just the scenery but the feeling of aloha which lingers like a fragrant scent.

Because it has so many aspects and dimensions, aloha is almost indefinable as these quotations show. Aloha is one of those intangibles that is hard to define yet one knows it when it is experienced or received. *The Book of Aloha* is a collection of definitions or explanations from Hawaiian scholars, authors, cultural practitioners and imminent personages—past and present—who explain in their own words what Aloha means to them and its importance in the Islands and beyond their shore to the entire world.

Live aloha, let aloha into your life, be aloha. This is the message of the wisdom in this collection.

In Hawaii we greet friends, loved ones
or strangers with Aloha, which means with love.
Aloha is the key word to the universal spirit of real
hospitality, which makes Hawai'i renowned as the
world's center of understanding and fellowship.
Try meeting or leaving people with Aloha.
You'll be surprised by their reaction.
I believe it and it is my creed. Aloha to you.

—Duke Kahanamoku

Honolulu Star-Bulletin, *John Titchen*

Aloha is the word that
extends the warmth, friendliness,
and pride of the Hawaiian people
to their islands' visitors.

—H. Thomas Steele

Honolulu Star-Bulletin, *Warren R. Roll*

The word *aloha,* in foreign use, has taken the place of every English equivalent. It is a greeting, a farewell, thanks, love, goodwill. *Aloha* looks at you from tidies and illuminations, it meets you on the roads and at house-doors, it is conveyed to you in letters, the air is full of it… It already represents to me all the kindness and goodwill that language can express…

—Isabella L. Bird

Hawaii and the Hawaiians are a land
and a people loving and lovable.
By their language may ye know them,
and in what other land save this one
is the commonest form of greeting,
not "Good day," nor "How d'ye do," but "Love"?
That greeting is *Aloha*—love, I love you, my love to you.
Good day—what is it more than an impersonal
remark about the weather? How do you do—
it is personal in a merely casual interrogative
sort of way. But Aloha! It is a positive
affirmation of the warmth of one's own heart-giving.
My love to you! I love you! Aloha!

—Jack London

Baker Van-Dyke Collection

Honolulu Star-Bulletin, *Jack Matsumoto*

Auwe! Auwe! Give me your hand.
Let me guide you to a place where the
sun is a burnished shield and the
moon is a disc of silver; where song
is the law of the land and a flower
has the importance of a garment.
Let me introduce you to my
Hawaiian friends whose word of greeting
and farewell is "Aloha," meaning love,
and the word is spoken with a gesture
which places a *lei,* a garland of gardenias,
orchids or silken-soft *plumeria*
about your shoulders.

—Don Blanding, 1930

And wherever he [the Native Hawaiian] went he said "Aloha" in meeting or in parting. "Aloha" was a recognition of life in another. If there was life there was *mana,* goodness and wisdom, and if there was goodness and wisdom there was a god-quality. One had to recognize the "god of life" in another before saying "Aloha," but this was easy. Life was everywhere—in the trees, the flowers, the ocean, the fish, the birds, the pili grass, the rainbow, the rock—in all the world was life—was god—was *aloha.*

—Helena G. Allen, author of *The Betrayal of Liliuokalani*

David Olsen

Arriving in Honolulu early in the spring of 1910, Liliuokalani was met at the wharf by *haole, hapa-haole,* and Hawaiians. She stepped off the ship with Curtis Iaukea and was greeted with "Alo-o-oha!"

Liliuokalani stopped, shocked, still. She stood unmoving until the cry melted away as if in chagrin. She looked down upon the crowd. "I greet you," she said in her rich musical voice, "with *aloha. Aloha*—that is the Hawaiian greeting." "Never," she told more than one Hawaiian child, including the adults such as Lydia, "never say *alo-o-oha*. It is a *haole* word. *Aloha* is ours, as is its meaning."

—Helena G. Allen, author of *The Betrayal of Liliuokalani*

Baker Van-Dyke Collection

The Hawaiian point of view is extremely valuable
and important to the community as a whole. For
example, all of us here in Hawaii, whether we have
Hawaiian blood or not, are proud of the fact that
we have aloha for each other and for strangers.

—E. S. C. Handy

Some modern Hawaiians believe that it was the most important of all ancient Hawaiian values. For example, the Reverend Akaiko Akana, for many years pastor of Kawaiaha'o Church until his death in 1932, stated, "Aloha, the very kernel of the Hawaiian ethics, the very core of the Hawaiian life, unsurpassed by anything of modern ethics, was the dominating law which regulated the domestic and civil conduct of old Hawai'i."

—George Hu'eu Sanford Kanahele

Hawai'i State Archives

Rob DeCamp

To greet the sun as it rises—
this was the tradition of the ancestors…
Everyone would turn to the sun with prayers of love
and gratitude because native practitioners believe
that with the coming of the sun and the *mana* [life force]
returns to Earth each day. With *mana* comes healing,
growth, life itself, for all creatures and the Earth.

—Lanakila Brandt

Honolulu Star-Bulletin, *Dennis Oda*

We are links to the ancients: connected by inheritance to their mana, their wisdom, their superb appreciation of what it is to be human. This is the foundation of the aloha spirit. It comes from many things, from knowing what it is to care, to truly care about other people.

—John Dominis Holt

My great-grandfather was born in the ancient way.
So I'm only four generations removed from a people who
lived in that time of truth. And now we are in a position
to give back to the world some of that ancient universal
wisdom. One way we do it is with Hawaiian music. In it
you hear the surf and see the rainbows and the
wind blowing the clouds across the sky.

—Kenny Brown

Shane Tegarden

In my view, aloha is not just a thought.
It is the path. It is the philosophical music of existence.
And for its sweet, harmonic presence in my life,
I am forever grateful.

—Keola Beamer

Honolulu Star-Bulletin, *Ken Sakamoto*

Shane Tegarden

All in all, it seems that the intensity of
Hawai'i's literature and its literary currents has
a lot to do with knowing a place, respecting and
caring for a place, and having Aloha for that place.
Just listen to the deep and poignant voice of Iz (Israel
Kamakawiwo'ole), a haunting voice that goes so deep
it gives you "chicken skin." Your hear it in the chants of
Charles Ka'upu. You see it in the stories told by the hands
of authentic hula dancers. You see it in the faces of
the homeless who walk our city streets.

—Rodney Morales

Shane Tegarden

"If you want to plan for one year, plant *kalo* [taro],"
a Hawaiian saying goes. "If you want to plan for ten years,
grow *koa*. If you want to plan for one hundred years,
teach the children."

—Puanani Burgess

Scott Mead

…the old folks always say every land, every stone is valuable because somehow it produces life. Put the land into use—let it feed us. *Aloha 'āina* [love of the land] means that. Nobody can save everything, otherwise we wouldn't have a place to be on these islands.

—Charley Keau

Ola ke kino i ka māʻona o ka ʻōpū.
I māʻona ka ʻōpū i ka mahiʻai o ka lima
a me ke aloha o nā kūpuna

The body is sustained by a full stomach.
A full stomach is attained by the hand of the farmer
and by the love of the elders.

—Tuti Kanahele

Douglas Peebles

Hawaiians feel *aloha* for Hawai'i from whence they come and for their Hawaiian kin upon whom they depend. It is nearly impossible to feel or practice *aloha* for something that is not familial. This is why we extend familial relations to those few non-Natives whom we feel understand and can reciprocate our *aloha*. But *aloha* is freely given and freely returned; it is not and cannot be demanded or commanded. Above all, *aloha* is a cultural feeling and practice that works among the people and between the people and their land.

—Haunani-Kay Trask

And there's something else I want to pass along
to this next generation of Hawaiian keiki:
'Imi au iā 'oe, e ke aloha.
Love brings us together as a family;
aloha brings us together as one.
You see, I've discovered that underneath,
we're all alike. We're all people like me.

—Danny Kaleikini

Honolulu Star-Bulletin, *Dennis Oda*

Baker Van-Dyke Collection

In the Hawai'i of my childhood, this feeling bonded the entire community. The whole village was your family; their sorrows became yours, and yours became theirs. We felt we were all related and could not help loving each other. As a child, I called our neighbors "uncle" or "tutu" or "auntie," a practice still observed by Hawaiian families today. We called it a calabash relationship, a word derived from the tradition we had of always sharing a great big calabash of poi that everybody dipped into, strangers and all. Eating from the same bowl, the same calabash—that is aloha.

—Nana Veary

Honolulu Star-Bulletin, *Amos Chun*

Aloha is when there is a room
with a million strangers and then they say "aloha,"
and then they are not strangers anymore.

—Makana, age 7

We are people from many different backgrounds
in the middle of God's Pacific—based on our Native
Hawaiian culture which bonds us together in a spirit of
love and pride, building upon those that came later for
a better life, reaching out so that their children's future
would be secure. Our E Pluribus Unum. All of this is
there for you to enjoy. To reinforce our nation's motto:
E Pluribus Unum. Out of the many, one. You see, to you,
from the community of communities to the nation
of nations, we bring you our spirit of *aloha*.

—Governor John Waihee, in his opening speech at the
1989 Festival of American Folklife in Washington, D.C.

Honolulu Star-Bulletin, *Ken Sakamoto*

49

Honolulu Star-Bulletin, *Jamm Aquino*

…aloha is special because it upholds,
reaffirms, and binds relationships.
Aloha should not be taken lightly.
It should not be used casually or frivolously.

—Malcolm Nāea Chun

Aloha is creative mutuality—turning clenched fists into
open arms and hands that reach out to embrace one
another, and to join in finding the best ways to build a
better world—then building it together.

—Senator Daniel Akaka in describing
Reverend Abraham K. Akaka's ministry

Honolulu Star-Bulletin, *unknown*

"Aloha ke Akua"—in other words, "God is Aloha."
Aloha is the power of God seeking to unite what is
separated in the world—the power that unites heart with
heart, soul with soul, life with life, culture with culture,
race with race, nation with nation.

—Reverend Abraham K. Akaka, from the Statehood Service
at Kawaiaha'o Church, 1959

Baker Van-Dyke Collection

I do put my love in my work because
this is what comes from my heart and I want to share it.
If you don't give what you have from your heart, sharing
all what you have, it don't mean anything.

—Elizabeth Lee, lauhala weaver

Quincy Dein

Hawaiians represent the compatibility of humans
and we have a responsibility to teach that—but without
preaching. Just watch us and we'll show you;
Let's go dance! Let's go surf!

To me, this is the secret and beauty of Hawai'i.
It's a marvelous, special place in the world. And
now we have the job of passing it along to others.
Because inside every one of us is a Hawaiian.

—Kenny Brown

Hawaiians were "hospitable, kindly, giving a welcome to strangers, affectionate, generous givers, who always invited strangers to sleep at the house and gave them food and fish without pay, and clothing for those who had little; a people ashamed to trade" (Kamakau, 1992, 201).

—Malcolm Nāea Chun

Baker Van-Dyke Collection

However else one defines *aloha,* as the beachboys embodied the concept it could be defined as "love freely, spontaneously, and generously given."

—Robert C. Allen

Though there are many disagreements within the native Hawaiian population and some strained relations among ethnic groups, there are some ideals which most people in Hawai'i strive for: *aloha*—which though overused in the commercial sense still is a powerful concept meaning love, affection, mercy, sympathy, kindness, sweetheart, and a greeting; and *ho'olokahi*—which means harmony or unity.

—Lynn Martin, Folk Arts Coordinator of the
Hawai'i State Foundation on Culture and the Arts, 1983-98

Honolulu Star-Bulletin, *Dennis Oda*

Monica and Michael Sweet

Lōkahi is mind, body and soul.
To just strengthen your physical self is not enough.
To strengthen yourself mentally is not enough.
To strengthen yourself spiritually is not enough.
To strengthen yourself physically, mentally
and spiritually is Lōkahi.

—Brian Keaulana

Quincy Dein

"Ua ola loko i ka aloha,"
"Love gives life within,"
a recognition that aloha is vital to one's
mental, emotional, and physical well-being.

—George Hu'eu Sanford Kanahele

When there's proper interaction, things are *pono*
[balanced]; there's appropriate *mana,* special kind of
power or energy maintaining this balance. These spiritual
inter-relationships are primary. Proper thoughts and
actions maintain this *pono,* harmony.

—Kekuni Blaisdell, M.D.

Honolulu Star-Bulletin, *Craig T. Kojima*

The state of aloha can be created in an instant.
It is a decision to behave with kindness, with generosity,
wanting to give joy to another.

—Auntie Irmgard Farden Aluli

In giving a *lei*, one shows respect
and love for someone else.

It isn't just a means of ornamenting the body. More
important, we make a *lei* and present it to honor our
fellow man….You do it with care, and care, to me, is
high regard for the person for whom you're making it.

—Marie McDonald

Honolulu Star-Bulletin, *Terry Luke*

Aloha is not just some words on a sign.
It's something you feel from inside.
So…I want to help you feel my Aloha.
I know you can feel it like me
It's here in your heart.

—"The Aloha Song" by Erika-Rae, Brooke Ligaya and Brother Noland

Honolulu Star-Bulletin, *Jamm Aquino*

Dennis Oda

What you learn in hula should go right to your heart.
You keep it there and you love it there. All the kumu hulas
I know, everything comes from the heart.

—Mae Akeo Brown

Let your feeling show in your face. Everything you feel, must show in your whole being. You must have aloha for it, understand it, before you can dance it.

—Helen Desha Beamer

Randy Jay Braun

"He kēhau hoʻomaʻemaʻe ke aloha,"
which compares love to "cleansing dew."
Like cleansing dew, the cleansing power of
aloha can sooth and even eliminate the pain
and hurt one may be suffering from.

—George Huʻeu Sanford Kanahele

Douglas Peebles

David Olsen

Another expression of love for the departed, which persists to this day, was the singing of songs that the person had loved, the chanting of *mele* that had been composed in honour of the person at birth, and the dancing of the several *hula* which dramatized these *mele*. This was a phase of Hawaiian custom entirely misunderstood by foreigners, especially early missionaries. To them it appeared an expression of "unseemly levity," whereas it was truly a token of *aloha*, for the *'uhane* would naturally be made happy by hearing and seeing those things that were loved throughout life.

—E. S. C. Handy and Mary Kawena Pukui

Honolulu Star-Bulletin, *unknown*

Aloha.
Needs must there be in every tongue,
Or roughly spoke, or sweetly sung,
A word of common greeting
That beareth oft repeating.

Bon dia, sayonara, or farewell,—
Spoke lightly, deeply, who can tell?
Adieu, good-bye, auf wiedersehn,—
The words are memory's refrain.

Aloha, dearest of them all,—
What pictures doth it not recall?
What tender tones in telling!
What sentiments upwelling!

Aloha,—'tis a loving cup;
With what thou wilt, thou fill'st it up.
A common dole to many lips,
Or chalice rare; one drinks or sips,
With love athirst or sated,
Sometimes with breath abated.

—Mary Dillingham Frear, 1915

"Aloha 'Oe," in its popular reception,
was transformed from a love song into
something quasi-elegiac…And, especially
in the tourist industry, the song now evokes a visitor's
sweetly sad departure from Hawai'i and promotes the
obvious wish that the visitor will return,
as the singer promises.

—Stephen H. Sumida

Steamer Day, Honolulu.

MATS NAVIGATION CO.

Bob Ebert

Aloha ʻOe

Haʻaheo ʻē ka ua i nā pali
Ke nihi aʻela i ka nahele
E uhai ana paha i ka liko
Pua ʻāhihi lehua o uka

Hui
Aloha ʻoe, aloha ʻoe,

E ke onaona noho i ka lipo.
One fond embrace, a hoʻi aʻe au
A hui hou aku.

ʻO ka haliʻa aloha ka i hiki mai
Ke hone aʻe nei i kuʻu manawa.
ʻO ʻoe nō kaʻu ipo aloha
A loko e hana nei.

Maopopo kuʻu ʻike i ka nani
Nā pua rose o Mauna-wili
I laila hoʻohie nā manu,
Mikiʻala i ka nani o ia pua.

Proudly the rain on the cliffs
Creeps into the forest
Seeking the buds.
And miniature lehua
  flowers of the uplands.

Chorus
Farewell to you, farewell to
  you,
O fragrance in the blue depths.
One fond embrace and I leave
To meet again.

Sweet memories come
Sound softly in my heart.
You are my beloved sweetheart
Felt within.

I understand the beauty
Of rose blossoms at Maunawili
There the birds delight,
Alert the beauty of this flower.

—Queen Liliʻuokalani

Contributors

Akaka, Reverend Abraham K.: The highly respected spiritual and civil rights leader who served at Kawaiaha'o Church from 1957-1984.

Akaka, Senator Daniel: The first U.S. Senator (1990-2011) of Native Hawaiian descent; author of the Akaka Bill to restore sovereignty to Native Hawaiians now awaiting action by the full U.S. Senate.

Allen, Helena G.: Author of *The Betrayal of Liliuokalani: Last Queen of Hawai'i; Kalakaua: Renaissance King;* and *Sanford Ballard Dole: Hawai'i's Only President.*

Allen, Robert C.: Active in shaping Hawai'i's tourism industry as director and president of numerous organizations including the Hawaii Vistors Bureau; author of *Creating Hawaii Tourism.*

Aluli, Irmgard Farden: Beloved songwriter, performer, and composer especially during the golden era of Hawaiian popular music.

Beamer, Helen Desha: One of Hawai'i's most influential musicians and hula dancers as well as the matriarch of the Beamer family of talented musicians, singers, composers, and dancers.

Beamer, Keola: Singer/songwriter, arranger/composer, and master slack-key guitarist whose musical talent springs from five generations of one of Hawai'i's most illustrious musical families.

Bird, Isabella L.: Nineteenth-century English explorer, writer, and natural historian whose visit to the Sandwich Islands in 1873 culminated with *Six Months in the Sandwich Islands: Among Hawai'i's Palm Groves, Coral Reefs, and Volcanoes.*

Blaisdell, Kekuni, M.D.: Physician, Native Hawaiian activist, and a founder of the University of Hawai'i's medical school.

Blanding, Don: A prolific poet whose writing captured 1920s Hawai'i.

Brandt, Lanakila: A kahuna pule (temple priest) of Pu'uhonua o Hōnaunau (Place of Refuge) on the Big Island, and a consecrated kahuna of the Mo'o Lono, or Order of Lord Lono.

Brown, Kenneth Francis (Kenny): Businessman, state senator (1968-74), architect, and visionary; the great-grandson of ali'i and historian, John Papa Ii, principal advisor to King Kamehameha IV.

Brown, Mae Akeo: Dancer and singer with the Kodak Hula Show for six decades, whose mother, Jenny Kealoha, sang with the Royal Hawaiian Band in the early twentieth century.

Burgess, Puanani: Native Hawaiian facilitator in community development, consultant, mediator, and poet, known for her work on the Waianae Coast.

Chun, Malcolm Nāea: Hawaiian culture specialist, teacher, educator, and author of books including *No Nā Mamo: Traditional and Contemporary Hawaiian Beliefs and Practices.*

Frear, Mary Dillingham: Daughter of industrialist Benjamin Dillingham, wife of former Territorial Governor William Frear; poet, author, and active in many community organizations.

Handy, Edward Smith Craighill, Ph.D.: Early twentieth-century ethnologist with the Bishop Museum.

Holt, John Dominis: Bishop Museum Trustee, publisher, and author whose 1964 essay "On Being Hawaiian" helped kindle the Hawaiian renaissance.

Kahanamoku, Duke: Olympic champion, Hollywood actor, surfing legend, and Ambassador of Aloha.

Kaleikini, Danny: Professional entertainer for over fifty years including headlining at the Kahala Hotel; proclaimed Ambassador of Aloha in 1988.

Kanahele, George Hu'eu Sanford: Civic leader, scholar, writer, and businessman whose work contributed to the Hawaiian renaissance.

Kanahele, Tuti: Ni'ihau kupuna whose past experience includes working with Alu Like, Inc., a nonprofit for Native Hawaiians, and teaching the Hawaiian language.

Keau, Charley: Archaeologist who worked in the 1970s-80s with Dr. Kenneth Emory restoring, studying, and preserving Maui cultural sites.

Keaulana, Brian: Professional surfer, lifeguard, skilled waterman, actor and stunt coordinator; son of legendary surfer Richard "Buffalo" Keaulana.

Lee, Elizabeth: Master lauhala weaver on the Kona Coast of the Big Island.

Lili'uokalani, Queen: Accomplished author, songwriter, and Hawai'i's last monarch, deposed during the 1893 overthrow of the Hawaiian Kingdom.

London, Jack: Author, journalist, and social activist who visited Hawai'i during the early twentieth century.

Martin, Lynn: Folk Arts Coordinator of the Hawai'i State Foundation on Culture and the Arts (1983-1998).

McDonald, Marie: Hawai'i's foremost lei authority and author of *Ka Lei: The Leis of Hawai'i*.

Morales, Rodney: University of Hawai'i English Professor and author of *When the Shark Bites* and *The Speed of Darkness*.

Noland, Brother: One of Hawai'i's musical icons, steward of the land, and community educator with The Tracking Project that connects individuals directly to the natural world.

Pukui, Mary Kawena: A Hawaiian scholar, dancer, composer, educator, and author whose numerous scholarly works have helped preserve the oral histories, proverbs, chants, songs, customs, and traditions of Hawaiians.

Steele, Thomas H.: Art director, author and designer of *The Hawaiian Shirt: Its Art and History*.

Sumida, Stephen H.: A pioneer in the field of Asian American studies, current Professor of American Ethnic Studies at the University of Washington, and author of *And the View from the Shore: Literary Traditions of Hawai'i*.

Trask, Haunani-Kay: Public speaker, indigenous leader, human rights organizer, and author of four books including *From a Native Daughter: Colonialism and Sovereignty in Hawai'i*.

Veary, Nana: Spiritual and inspirational leader, "Living Treasure" (declared by the Hawai'i State Legislature before her passing), and author of the seminal book *Change We Must*.

Waihee, Governor John: Fourth governor of Hawai'i (1986-1994) and the first governor of Native Hawaiian ancestry; instrumental in the creation of the Office of Hawaiian Affairs in 1978.

Sources

Page 6   Hall, Sandra Kimberley. *Duke: A Great Hawaiian*. Honolulu: Bess Press, 2004.

Page 8   Steele, H. Thomas. *The Hawaiian Shirt: Its Art and History*. Bloomington: Abbeville Press, 1984.

Page 11   Bird, Isabella L. *Six Months in the Sandwich Islands Among Hawai'i's Palm Groves, Coral Reefs, and Volcanoes* . New York: G.P. Putnam's Sons, 1881.

Page 12   London, Jack. *Stories of Hawaii*. Honolulu: Mutual Publishing, 1986.

Page 15   Blanding, Don. *Hula Moons*. New York: Dodd, Mead & Company, 1930.

Page 16, 18   Allen, Helena G. *The Betrayal of Liliuokalani: Last Queen of Hawaii 1838-1917*. Honolulu: Mutual Publishing, 1982.

Page 21   Handy, E.S.C. *Ancient Hawaiian Civilization*. Honolulu: Mutual Publishing, 1999.

Page 22, 67 (top), 78   Kanahele, George Hu'eu Sanford. *Kū Kanaka: Stand Tall, A Search for Hawaiian Values*. Honolulu: University of Hawai'i Press, 1986.

Page 25, 37, 55, 67 (bottom), 70   Harden, M.J. *Voices of Wisdom: Hawaiian Elders Speak*. Kula: Aka Press, 1999.

Page 27   Holt, John Dominis. *On Being Hawaiian*. Honolulu: Ku Pa'a Publishing, 1995.

Page 28, 57, 72, 75   Hiura, Arnold and Engebretson, George, eds. *The Lessons of Aloha: Stories of the Human Spirit with Brother Noland*. Honolulu: Watermark Publishing, 1999.

Page 30   Ellman, Mark and Santos, Barbara, eds. *Practice Aloha: Secrets to Living Life Hawaiian Style*. Honolulu: Mutual Publishing, 2010.

Page 33   Haas, Michael, ed. *Barack Obama, The Aloha Zen President: How a Son of the 50th State May Revitalize America Based on 12 Multicultural Principles.* Santa Barbara: ABC-CLIO, LLC, 2011.

Page 35   Fujii, Jocelyn. *Stories of Aloha: Homegrown Treasures of Hawai'i.* Honolulu: Hula Moon Press, 2009.

Page 38   Meahl, Elizabeth, ed. *Alu Like's Healthy Local Recipes for Hawai'i's Kūpuna.* Honolulu: Mutual Publishing, 2003.

Page 41   Trask, Haunani-Kay. *From a Native Daughter: Colonialism and Sovereignty in Hawai'i.* Honolulu: University of Hawai'i Press, 1999.

Page 42, 45, 47, 69   Canfield, Jack; Hansen, Mark Victor; Linnéa, Sharon; and Roher, Robin Stephens, eds. *Chicken Soup from the Soul of Hawai'i: Stories of Aloha to Create Paradise Wherever You Are.* Deerfield Beach: Health Communications, Inc., 2003.

Page 48, 62   Diamond, Heather A. *American Aloha: Cultural Tourism and the Negotiation of Tradition.* Honolulu: University of Hawai'i Press, 2008.

Page 51 (top), 58   Chun, Malcolm Nāea. *Aloha: Traditions of Love and Affection: Ka Wana Series, Book 12.* Honolulu: University of Hawai'i Press, 2011.

Page 51 (bottom)   Senator Daniel Akaka describing the Reverend Abraham Kahikina Akaka's, ministry. http://akaka.senate.gov/statements-and-speeches.cfm?method=releases.view&id=9fb7e9de-f988-47b7-aa3d-ae1678e1d356.

Page 53   Reverend Abraham Kahikina Akaka from the Statehood Service delivered at Kawaiaha'o Church on March 13, 1959, the day after statehood was announced. www.akakafoundation.org/tribute.html

Page 60   Allen, Robert C. *Creating Hawai'i Tourism: A Memoir.* Honolulu: Bess Press, 2004.

Page 65   *Surfing: He'e Nalu, Hawaiian Proverbs & Inspirational Quotes Celebrating Hawai'i's Royal Sport.* Honolulu: Mutual Publishing, 2003.

Page 76   Hopkins, Jerry. *The Hula*. Apa Productions, 1982.

Page 81   Handy, E.S. Craighill and Pukui, Mary Kawena. T*he Polynesian Family System in Ka'u,* Hawai'i. Honolulu: Mutual Publishing, 1998.

Page 83   Schnack, Ferdinand J.H. *The Aloha Guide: The Standard Handbook of Honolulu and the Hawaiian Islands, For Travelers and Residents with a Historical Resume, Illustrations and Maps.* Honolulu: *Honolulu Star-Bulletin,* 1915.

Page 84, 86   Sumida, Stephen H. *And the View from the Shore: Literary Traditions of Hawai'i.* Seattle: University of Washington Press, 1991.